AUTISTICALLY ME

By ROBERT J. MOORE

Illustrations by Spoiled Graphics

AUTISTICALLY ME

ROBERT J MOORE

ILLUSTRATED BY SPOILED GRAPHICS

1

SOMETIMES PEOPLE STARE AT ME, WHISPER, OR EVEN LAUGH. BUT GUESS WHAT? I'M NOT WORRIED. YOU SEE, I'M JUST AUTISTICALLY ME.

2

WHEN I WALK INTO A ROOM, I NOTICE EVERYTHING—THE BRIGHT LIGHTS, THE SOUNDS THAT BUZZ, AND THE COLORS ALL AROUND.

SOMETIMES,
I MIGHT COVER MY EARS OR
CLOSE MY EYES. IT'S NOT
BECAUSE I'M SCARED OR
SHY. I JUST FEEL THE WORLD
A LITTLE DIFFERENTLY
THAN MOST.

YOU MAY THINK I AM DIFFERENT, HUH? I SEE, BUT NOPE! I'M JUST AUTISTICALLY ME. PEOPLE ARE POINTING FINGERS, STARING, LOOKING AT ME —BUT YOU THINK WE DON'T SEE. I AM UNIQUELY MADE BY GOD, YET DIFFERENT, BUT FREE.

FREE TO BE ME.
FREE TO DO THINGS YOU SOON WON'T BELIEVE! LIKE THE TIME I TOOK APART A COMPUTER—EVERY SINGLE PIECE!—AND THEN PUT IT BACK TOGETHER ALL BY MYSELF. OR HOW I CAN

PLAY VIDEO GAMES WITH MY FRIENDS AND SOMETIMES EVEN BEAT THEM. OH, AND DID I MENTION SPORTS? YEP, I CAN DO THAT TOO!

MAYBE I'M NOT THE FASTEST RUNNER, BUT I SURE KNOW HOW TO KICK A BALL AND MAKE A GOAL.

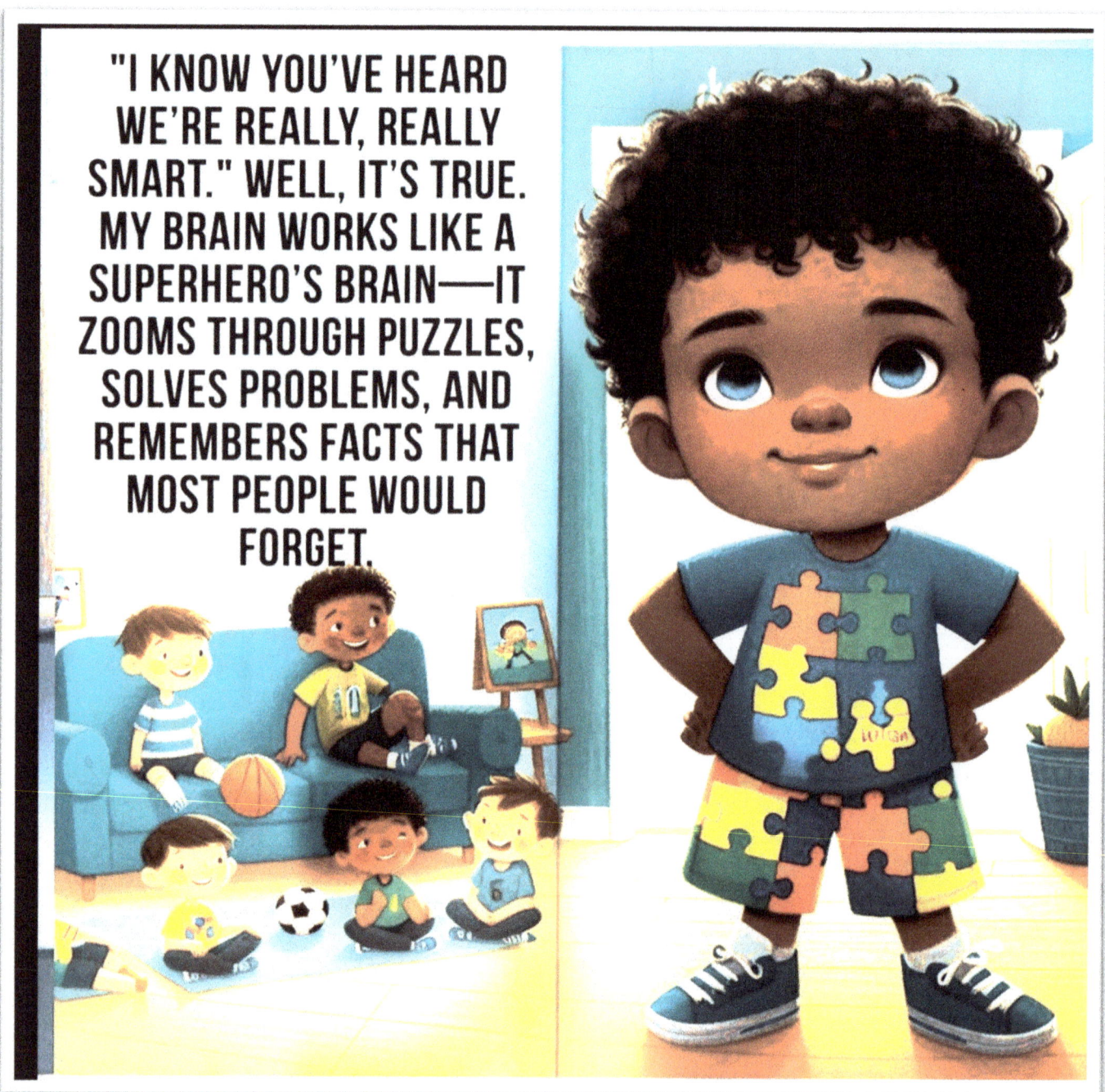

"I KNOW YOU'VE HEARD WE'RE REALLY, REALLY SMART." WELL, IT'S TRUE. MY BRAIN WORKS LIKE A SUPERHERO'S BRAIN——IT ZOOMS THROUGH PUZZLES, SOLVES PROBLEMS, AND REMEMBERS FACTS THAT MOST PEOPLE WOULD FORGET.

LIKE HOW MANY STARS ARE IN THE SKY? I COULD TELL YOU! OR HOW LONG IT TAKES FOR A ROCKET TO BLAST OFF INTO SPACE. I MIGHT EVEN SHOW YOU ONE DAY.

I am Jay ....

SO, THE NEXT TIME YOU SEE SOMEONE LIKE ME, JUST REMEMBER:

WE MAY NOT DO THINGS THE SAME WAY YOU DO, BUT THAT'S OKAY. I'M STILL JAY. I'M STILL FUN, CARING, AND STRONG.

BECAUSE EVEN IF I'M DIFFERENT, I'M ALSO THE SAME IN MANY WAYS. I HAVE DREAMS, HOPES, AND TONS OF LOVE TO GIVE. I MIGHT TAKE THE LONG WAY TO GET THERE,

BUT I'LL ALWAYS REACH FOR THE STARS. I UNIQUELY MADE BY GOD JUST LIKE YOU. READY TO SHOW THE WORLD ALL THE INCREDIBLE THINGS I CAN DO

I AM JAY. I AM PROUD. AND I AM FOREVER ME...

AUTISTIC THAT'S RIGHT... AUTISICALLY ME.

12

ACKNOWLEDGMENTS

I wrote *Autistically Me* because of two incredible boys who changed my life forever. When I married their mother, I had the blessing and honor of helping raise her twin sons, both of whom are on the autism spectrum. I met them when they were just four years old, on the verge of starting kindergarten. From that moment on, I became deeply involved in their lives—attending doctors' appointments, school events, and sports activities. Being a stepfather to two superheroes wasn't always easy, but it was one of the most rewarding and beautiful experiences of my life. These boys brought me so much joy, laughter, and unforgettable memories that I carry with me every day.

DEDICATIONS

This book is especially dedicated to Jay, one of the twins and the inspiration behind the main character. Jay is a special kid, and our bond was unlike anything I've ever experienced. I'll never forget the way he used to come into my room in the mornings and ask, "Good morning, Coach Rob, are you still going to be my protector?" That simple question meant everything to me. Even when he drove me a little crazy, I missed him the moment he wasn't around. Though it's been almost two years since I left the home we all shared, my love for Jay and his brother has never faded. People and relationships may come and go, but those boys will always have a permanent place in my heart. I wrote this book to honor them—and to remind every child like Jay that they are uniquely made, deeply loved, and wonderfully free to be themselves.

13

AUTISTICALLY ME

By Robert J. Moore

Illustrations: **Spoiled Graphics**

Editor: Anelda Attaway

Published by Jazzy Kitty Publications

Wilmington, Delaware

877.782.5550 - http://www.jazzykittypublications.com

anelda@jazzykittypublications.com

Copyright © 2025 Robert J. Moore

ISBN 978-1-965381-11-3

ME & THE TWINS

15

Autism Spectrum Disorder

It is a condition related to brain development that affects how people see others and socialize with them. This can cause problems in communication and social interaction with others. The condition also includes limited and repeated patterns of behavior. The term "Spectrum" in Autism Spectrum Disorder refers to the wide range of symptoms and the severity of these symptoms.

Autism Spectrum Disorder includes conditions that were once thought to be separate — Autism, Asperger's Syndrome, Childhood Disintegrative Disorder, and a form of widespread developmental disorder that isn't specified, which begins in early childhood. Over time, it can cause difficulty functioning in society.

For example, people with Autism may have problems being social, or when in school, or at work. Often, children show symptoms of Autism within the first year of life. A small number of children with the condition appear to develop as expected in the first year. Then, between 18 and 24 months of age, they may lose some skills and develop autism symptoms. There is no cure for autism spectrum disorder. But getting treatment early, during the preschool years, can make a big difference in the lives of many children with the condition.

Symptoms

Children show signs of autism spectrum disorder in early infancy, such as less eye contact, not responding to their names, or not being interested in caregivers. Other children may not develop as expected for the first few months or years of life. Then they suddenly become withdrawn or aggressive or lose the language skills they had before.

Signs usually are seen in the ages 2 to 3 years old. Because each child can have a unique mix of symptoms, sometimes it can be hard to tell how severe the condition is. It's generally based on how severe the symptoms are and how much those symptoms affect a child with the ability to function.

www.ingramcontent.com/pod-product-compliance
Lightning Source LLC
Chambersburg PA
CBHW051629140626
46547CB00033B/2987